Tomie dePaola's
Book of
CHRISTMAS CAROLS

SIMON & SCHUSTER
BOOKS FOR YOUNG READERS

NEW YORK   LONDON   TORONTO   SYDNEY   NEW DELHI

For Tony Parisi,
who directed the Special Chorus at Meriden
High School and brought much Christmas joy to
the entire city with the Annual Christmas Sing

English translation of *'Twas in the Moon of Wintertime* used by permission of
The Frederick Harris Music Co., Limited, Oakville, Ontario, Canada.

SIMON & SCHUSTER BOOKS FOR YOUNG READERS
An imprint of Simon & Schuster Children's Publishing Division
1230 Avenue of the Americas, New York, New York 10020
© 1987 by Tomie dePaola
Book design by Laurent Linn © 2022 by Simon & Schuster, Inc.
Music typesetting by Music Book Associates, Inc.
Music consultation by Susan Friedlander
SIMON & SCHUSTER BOOKS FOR YOUNG READERS and related marks are trademarks of Simon & Schuster, Inc.
For information about special discounts for bulk purchases, please contact Simon & Schuster Special Sales
at 1-866-506-1949 or business@simonandschuster.com.
The Simon & Schuster Speakers Bureau can bring authors to your live event. For more information or to book an event,
contact the Simon & Schuster Speakers Bureau at 1-866-248-3049 or visit our website at www.simonspeakers.com.
The text for this book was set in Baskerville Regular.
Manufactured in China
0622 SCP
First Simon & Schuster Books for Young Readers hardcover edition October 2022
2 4 6 8 10 9 7 5 3 1
ISBN 9781534494855
ISBN 9781534494862 (ebook)

CONTENTS

Villagers all, this frosty tide,
Let your doors swing open wide,
Though wind may follow, and snow beside,
Yet draw us in by your fire to bide;
Joy shall be yours in the morning!

Carol from *Wind in the Willows*

O Come, O Come, Emmanuel

Translated by John Mason Neale

Gregorian

Freely

O come, O come, Em - man - u - el, And ran - som cap - tive Is - ra - el,

That mourns in lone - ly ex - ile here, Un - til the Son of God___ ap - pear.

Refrain

Re - joice! Re - joice! Em - man - u - el Shall come to thee, O Is - ra - el.

The First Noël

Traditional

16th century French

Moderately

1. The__ first__ No - ël the__ an - gels did say Was to
2. They__ look - èd__ up and__ saw__ a star Shin - ing

cer - tain poor shep - herds in fields as they lay; In__ fields__ where they lay__
in__ the east__ be - yond__ them far, And__ to__ the__ earth it__

keep - ing their sheep On a cold win -ter's night___ that was___ so deep.
gave___ great light, And___ so it con -tin -ued both day___ and night.

Refrain

No - ël,___ No - ël, No - ël, No - ël,___ Born is the King of Is - ra -el.

While Shepherds Watched Their Flocks by Night

Winchester Old

Adapted from George F. Handel

Tenderly

1. While shep-herds watch'd their flocks by night, All seat-ed on the ground, The an-gel of the Lord came down, And glory shone a-round, And glory shone a-round.

2. "Fear not!" said he for might-y dread Had seized their troub-led mind; "Glad ti-dings of great joy I bring To you and all man-kind, To you and all man-kind."

3. "To you, in David's town this day,
   Is born of David's line
   The Savior, who is Christ the Lord;
   And this shall be the sign:

4. "The heav'nly Babe you there shall find,
   To human view displayed,
   All meanly wrapp'd in swathing bands,
   And in a manger laid."

5. Thus spake the seraph, and forthwith
   Appear'd a shining throng
   Of angels praising God, who thus
   Address'd their joyful song:

6. "All glory be to God on high,
   And to the earth be peace;
   Good will henceforth from heav'n to men
   Begin and never cease."

It Came Upon the Midnight Clear

Edmund H. Sears, 1850

Richard S. Willis, 1851

1. It came up-on__ the mid-night clear, That glo-rious song__ of old,__
2. Still thro' the clo-ven skies they come, With peace-ful wings un-furled;

From an-gels bend-ing near the earth To touch their harps__ of gold:__
And still their heav'n-ly mu-sic floats O'er all the wear-y world:__

"Peace on the earth,__ good will to men, From heav'n's all gra-cious King,"
A-bove its sad__ and low-ly plains They bend__ on hove-ring wing;__

The world in sol-emn still-ness lay To hear the an-gels sing.__
And ev-er o'er__ its Ba-bel sounds The bless-èd an-gels sing.__

Once in Royal David's City

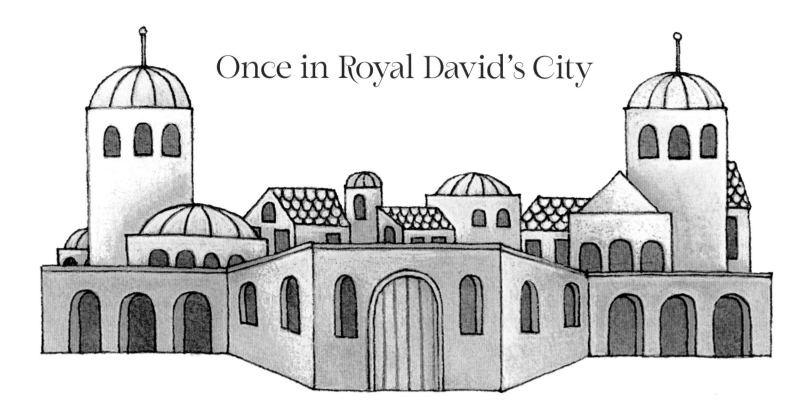

Cecil Frances Alexander

Henry J. Gauntlett
Arranged by A. H. Mann

Broadly

1. Once in roy - al Dav - id's ci - ty Stood a low - ly cat - tle shed,
2. He came down to earth from hea - ven, Who is God and Lord of all,
3. Not in that poor low - ly sta - ble, With the ox - en stand - ing by,

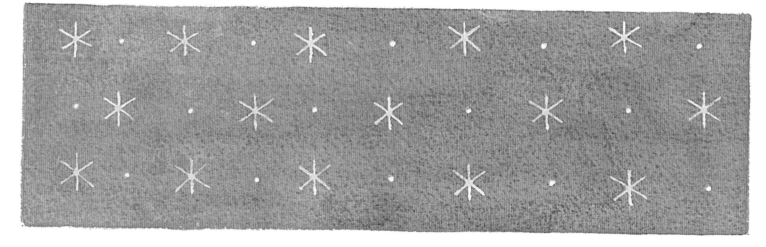

Where a moth-er laid__ her__ ba - by In a man-ger for__ His__ bed;
And His shel-ter was__ a__ sta - ble, And His cra - dle was__ a__ stall;
We shall see Him; but in__ hea - ven, Set at God's right hand on__ high;

Ma - ry was that moth__er mild,__ Je - sus Christ her lit - tle__ child.__
With the poor, and mean, and low - ly, Lived on earth our Sav - ior__ ho - ly.
When like stars His chil - dren crowned All in white shall wait a - round.__

Silent Night

Joseph Möhr, 1818

Franz Grüber, 1818

Tenderly

1. Si - lent night! Ho - ly night! All is calm, all is bright.
2. Si - lent night! Ho - ly night! Shep - herds quake at the sight!
3. Si - lent night! Ho - ly night! Son of God, love's pure light!

'Round yon vir - gin moth - er and child! Ho - ly In - fant, so ten - der and mild,
Glo - ries stream_ from heav - en a - far, Heav'n - ly hosts_ sing, "Al - le - lu - ia!"
Ra - diant beams_ from Thy ho - ly face, With the dawn of re - deem - ing grace,

Sleep in heav - en - ly peace,_ Sleep_ in heav - en - ly peace._
Christ, the Sav - ior, is born!_ Christ,_ the Sav - ior, is born!_
Je - sus, Lord, at Thy birth,_ Je - sus, Lord, at Thy birth._

Angels We Have Heard on High

Traditional

Old French Melody

Joyously

1. An - gels we have heard on high, Sweet - ly sing - ing o'er the plains;
2. Shep - herds, why this ju - bi - lee? Why your joy - ous strains pro - long?
3. Come to Beth - le - hem, and see Him whose birth the an - gels sing;

And the moun - tains in re - ply Ech - o - ing their joy - ous strains.
What the glad - some ti - dings be Which in - spire your heaven - ly song?
Come a - dore on bend - ed knee, Christ, the Lord, the new - born King.

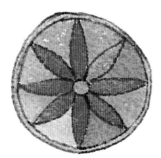

Rise Up, Shepherd, and Follow

Moderately fast

Black Spiritual

1. There's a star in the East on__ Christ-mas morn, Rise up, shep-herd, and fol-low,
2. If you take good__ heed to the an-gel's words, Rise up, shep-herd, and fol-low,

It'-ll lead to the place where the Sav-ior's born,__ Rise up, shep-herd, and fol-low.
You'll for-get your flocks, you'll for-get your herds,__ Rise up, shep-herd, and fol-low.

The Friendly Beasts

3. "I," said the cow, all white and red,
   "I gave Him my manger for His bed;
   I gave Him my hay to pillow His head;
   I," said the cow, all white and red.

4. "I," said the sheep with curly horn,
   I gave Him my wool for His blanket warm,
   He wore my coat on Christmas morn.
   I," said the sheep with curly horn.

5. "I," said the dove from the rafters high,
   Cooed Him to sleep, that He should not cry,
   We cooed Him to sleep, my mate and I.
   I," said the dove from the rafters high.

6. Thus every beast by some good spell,
   In the stable dark was glad to tell
   Of the gift he gave Emmanuel,
   The gift he gave Emmanuel.

What Child Is This?

Hark! The Herald Angels Sing

Charles Wesley, 1739

Felix Mendelssohn, 1840
Arranged by W. H. Cummings, 1855

Joyfully

1. Hark! the her-ald an-gels sing,__ "Glo-ry to the__ new-born King,
2. Christ, by high-est heav'n a-dored, Christ, the ev-er-last-ing Lord;

Peace on earth, and mer-cy mild,__ God and sin-ners re-con-ciled."
Late in time be-hold Him come,__ Off-spring of the fa-vored one.

Joy-ful, all ye na-tions, rise,__ Join the tri-umph of the skies;__
Veiled in flesh, the God-head see!__ Hail, th'in-car-nate De-i-ty!__

Away in a Manger

Anonymous

15th century German
Arranged by Nick Nicholson

Softly

1. A - way in a man - ger, no crib for a bed, The
2. The cat - tle are low - ing, the poor ba - by wakes, But

lit - tle Lord Je - sus laid down His sweet head, The
lit - tle Lord Je - sus, no cry - ing He makes, I

stars in the sky,⎯ looked down where He lay, The
love Thee, Lord Je - sus, look down from the sky, And

lit - tle Lord Je - sus, a - sleep on the hay.
stay by my cra - dle, till morn - ing is nigh.

The Coventry Carol

Robert Croo, 1534

English Melody, 1591
Arranged by Nick Nicholson

Slowly, tenderly

1. Lul - lay, Thou lit - tle ti - ny Child, Bye, bye, lul - ly, lul - lay;___
2. O sis - ters, too, how may we do, For to pre - serve this day;___

Lul - lay, Thou lit - tle ti - ny Child, Bye, bye, lul - ly, lul - lay.___
This poor Young - ling for whom we sing, Bye, bye, lul - ly, lul - lay.___

3. Herod the King, in his raging,
    Charged he hath this day;
    His men of might, in his own sight,
    All children young to slay.

4. Then woe is me, poor Child, for thee,
    And ever mourn and say;
    For thy parting nor say nor sing,
    Bye, bye lully, lullay.

5. *Repeat verse 1.*

I Heard the Bells on Christmas Day

Henry W. Longfellow, 1863

J. Baptiste Calkin, 1872

Robustly

1. I heard the bells on Christmas day Their old familiar carols play,
2. I thought how, as the day had come, The belfries of all Christendom
3. And in despair I bow'd my head: "There is no peace on earth," I said,

And wild and sweet the words repeat Of peace on earth, good will to men.
Had roll'd along th'unbroken song Of peace on earth, good will to men.
"For hate is strong and mocks the song Of peace on earth, good will to men."

4. Then pealed the bells more loud and deep:
   "God is not dead, nor doth He sleep;
   The wrong shall fail, the right prevail,
   With peace on earth, good will to men."

5. Till, ringing, singing on its way,
   The world revolv'd from night to day,
   A voice, a chime, a chant sublime,
   Of peace on earth, good will to men!

Lo, How a Rose E'er Blooming

Old German
Translated by Theodore Baker

15th century German
Michael Praetorious, 1609

Joyfully

1. Lo, how a Rose e'er bloom - ing From ten - der
2. I - sa - iah 'twas fore - told it, The Rose I had

stem hath sprung! Of Jes - se's lin - eage com - ing As men of
in mind, With Ma - ry we be - hold it, The Vir - gin Moth -

old have sung. It came, a flow'r - et bright, A - mid the
- er kind. To show God's love a - right She bore to

cold of win - ter, When half___ spent___ was the night.
men a Sav - ior, When half___ spent___ was the night.

I Saw Three Ships

Traditional

Arranged by Sir John Stainer

O Come, All Ye Faithful

ADESTE, FIDELES

17th century Latin
Translated by F. Oakeley, 1852

Wade, 1751

Steadily

1. O come, all ye faith-ful, Joy-ful and tri-umph-ant, O
1. *Ad - es - te, fi - de - les, Lae - ti tri - um - phan - tes, Ve -*
2. — Sing choirs of An - gels, Sing in ex - ul - ta - tion,—

come ye, O come__ ye to Beth - le - hem;
ni - te, ve - ni - te in Beth - le - hem;
Sing all ye cit - i - zens of heav'n__ a - bove:

Come and be - hold Him, Born the King of An - gels:
Na - tum vi - de - te, Re - gem an - ge - lo - rum:
Glo - ry to God____ in____ the____ high - est:

O come, let us a - dore Him, O come, let us a - dore Him,
Ve - ni - te a - do - re - mus, Ve - ni - te a - do - re - mus,
O come, let us a - dore Him, O come, let us a - dore Him,

O come, let us a - dore Him, Christ, the Lord.
Ve - ni - te a - do - re - mus, Do - mi - num.
O come, let us a - dore Him, Christ, the Lord.

O Little Town of Bethlehem

Phillips Brooks, 1868

Lewis H. Redner, 1868

Tenderly

1. O lit - tle town of Beth - le - hem, How still we see thee lie!
2. For Christ is born of Ma - ry; And, gath - ered all a - bove,

A - bove thy deep and dream - less sleep The si - lent stars go by:
While mor - tals sleep, the an - gels keep Their watch of won - dering love.

Yet in thy dark streets shin - eth The ev - er - last - ing Light;
O morn - ing stars, to - geth - er Pro - claim the ho - ly birth;

The hopes and fears of all the years Are met in thee to - night.
And prais - es sing to God, the King, And peace to men on earth.

3. How silently, how silently,
   The wondrous gift is given!
   So God imparts to human hearts
   The blessings of His heaven.
   No ear may hear His coming;
   But in this world of sin,
   Where meek souls will receive Him, still
   The dear Christ enters in.

4. O holy Child of Bethlehem,
   Descend to us, we pray;
   Cast out our sin, and enter in;
   Be born in us today.
   We hear the Christmas angels
   The great glad tidings tell;
   O come to us, abide with us,
   Our Lord Emmanuel.

We Three Kings of Orient Are

John H. Hopkins, Jr., 1857

John H. Hopkins, Jr.

Moderately

1. We three kings of O - ri - ent are, Bear - ing gifts we trav - erse a -
2. Born a babe on Beth - le - hem's plain, Gold we bring to crown Him a -

far, Field and foun - tain, moor and moun - tain, Fol - low - ing yon - der Star.
gain; King for - ev - er, ceas - ing nev - er, O - ver us all to reign.

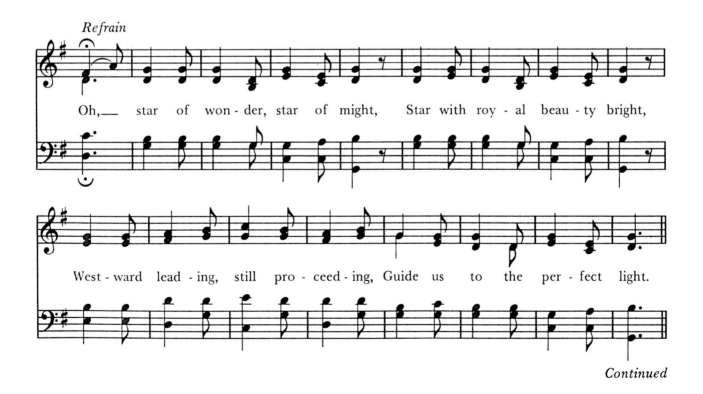

Refrain

Oh,— star of won-der, star of might, Star with roy-al beau-ty bright,

West-ward lead-ing, still pro-ceed-ing, Guide us to the per-fect light.

Continued

3. Frank - in - cense to of - fer have I; In - cense owns a De - i - ty
4. Myrrh is mine; its bit - ter per - fume Breathes a life of gath - er - ing
5. Glo - rious now be - hold— Him rise, King and God and Sac - ri -

nigh, **Pray'r** and prais - ing all men rais - ing, Wor - ship God on high.
gloom; Sor - row - ing, sigh - ing, bleed - ing, dy - ing, Sealed in the stone - cold tomb.
fice; Heav'n sings "Hal - le - lu - jah!" "Hal - le - lu - jah!" earth re - plies.

Oh,— star of won-der, star of might, Star with roy-al beau-ty bright,

West-ward lead-ing, still pro-ceed-ing, Guide us to the per-fect light.

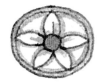 

Joy to the World!

Isaac Watts, 1719

George F. Handel, 1742
Arranged by Lowell Mason, 1830

God Rest You Merry, Gentlemen

Traditional

English Carol
Arranged by Sir John Stainer

Joyfully

1. God rest you mer - ry, gen - tle - men, Let noth - ing you dis - may,
2. In Beth - le - hem, in Jew - ry, This bless - ed Babe was born,
3. From God, our heav'n - ly Fa - ther, A bless - ed an - gel came,

Re - mem - ber, Christ, our Sav - ior, Was born on Christ - mas day;
And laid with - in a man - ger Up - on this bless - ed morn;
And un - to cer - tain shep - herds Brought ti - dings of the same;

To save us all from Sa - tan's pow'r, When we were gone a - stray.
The which His moth - er Ma - ry Did noth - ing take in scorn.
How that in Beth - le - hem was born The Son of God by name.

The Holly and the Ivy

Traditional

English
Arranged by Allen L. Richardson

1. The hol-ly and the i-vy, When they are both full grown,
2. The hol-ly bears a blos-som, As white as the li-ly flow'r,
3. The hol-ly bears a ber-ry, As red as an-y blood,

Of all the trees that are in the wood, The hol-ly bears the crown:
And Ma-ry bore sweet Je-sus Christ, To be our sweet Sa-vior:
And Ma-ry bore sweet Je-sus Christ, To do poor sin-ners good:

Refrain

The ris-ing of the sun And the run-ning of the deer,

The play-ing of the mer-ry or-gan, Sweet sing-ing in the choir.

Deck the Halls

Traditional

Old Welsh Air

Spirited

1. Deck the halls with boughs of hol - ly,
2. See the blaz - ing Yule be - fore us,
3. Fast a - way the old year pass - es,

Fa la la la la, la la la la.

'Tis the sea - son to be jol - ly,
Strike the harp and join the cho - rus,
Hail the new, ye lads and lass - es,

Fa la la la la, la la la la.

Don we now our gay ap - par - el,
Fol - low me in mer - ry mea - sure, } Fa la la la la la la la la,
Sing we joy - ous all to - geth - er,

Troll the an - cient Yule - tide car - ol,
While I tell of Yule - tide treas - ure, } Fa, la, la, la, la, la, la, la, la.
Heed - less of the wind and weath - er,

Bring a Torch, Jeannette, Isabella!

UN FLAMBEAU, JEANNETTE, ISABELLE!

Traditional French
Translated by Edward Cuthbert Nunn

17th century Old French
Attributed to Saboly

Lively

1. Bring a torch,___ Jean - nette, Is - a - bel - la!
1. Un flam - beau,___ Jean - nette, Is - a - bel - le,

Bring a torch, to the cra - dle run! It is
Un flam - beau,___ cou - rons au ber - ceau! C'est Jé -

Je - sus, good folk of the vil - lage; Christ___ is born and
sus, bon nes gens du ha - meau,___ Le Christ est né, Mar -

Ma - ry's call - ing: Ah! ah! beau - ti - ful is the
ie ap - pel - le, Ah! ah! que___ la mère est

Moth - er! Ah! ah! beau - ti - ful is her Son!___
bel - le, Ah! ah! ah! que l'En - fant est beau!___

Good King Wenceslas

John Mason Neale

Traditional
Arranged by Sir John Stainer

Robustly

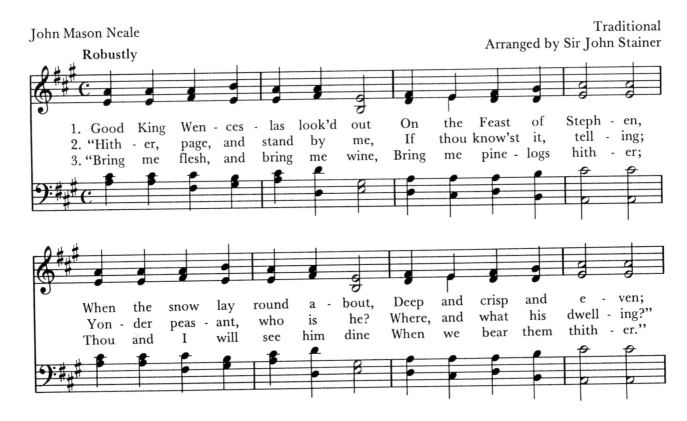

1. Good King Wen - ces - las look'd out On the Feast of Steph - en,
2. "Hith - er, page, and stand by me, If thou know'st it, tell - ing;
3. "Bring me flesh, and bring me wine, Bring me pine - logs hith - er;

When the snow lay round a - bout, Deep and crisp and e - ven;
Yon - der peas - ant, who is he? Where, and what his dwell - ing?"
Thou and I will see him dine When we bear them thith - er."

O Christmas Tree

O TANNENBAUM

German Folk Song

Moderately

1. O Christ-mas tree, O Christ-mas tree, For-ev-er green your branch-es!
1. O Tan-nen-baum, O Tan-nen-baum, Wie treu sind dei-ne Blät-ter!
2. And, oh, the Christ-mas tree can be A source of sim-ple plea-sure:

How full and fair in sum-mer's glow, And thick and green in win-ter's snow.
Du grünst nicht nur zur Som-mers-zeit, Nein, auch im Win-ter, wenn es schneit.
To ev-ery girl and ev-ery boy It speaks of hol-i-days and joy:

O Christ-mas tree, O Christ-mas tree, For-ev-er green your branch-es!
O Tan-nen-baum, O Tan-nen-baum, Wie treu sind dei-ne Blät-ter!
Ah yes, the Christ-mas tree can be A source of sim-ple plea-sure.

Bright - ly shone the moon that night, Tho' the frost was cru - el,
"Sire, he lives a good league hence, Un - der - neath the moun - tain;
Page and mon - arch forth they went, Forth they went to - geth - er;

When a poor man came in sight, Gath - 'ring win - ter fu - el.
Right a - gainst the for - est fence, By Saint Ag - nes' foun - tain."
Thro' the rude wind's wild la - ment And the bit - ter weath - er.

4. "Sire, the night is darker now,
 And the wind blows stronger;
 Fails my heart, I know not how,
 I can go no longer."

"Mark my footsteps, my good page,
Tread thou in them boldly:
Thou shalt find the winter's rage
Freeze thy blood less coldly."

5. In his master's steps he trod,
 Where the snow lay dinted;
 Heat was in the very sod
 Which the saint had printed;

Therefore, Christian men, be sure,
Wealth or rank possessing,
Ye who now will bless the poor,
Shall yourselves find blessing.

The Cherry Tree Carol

English

Traditional

Sweetly

1. __ Jo - seph was an old __ man, An old man was __ he:
2. As Jo - seph and __ Ma - ry were walk - ing one __ day,
3. Then Ma - ry said to Jo - seph, so meek and so __ mild,

He __ mar - ried Vir - gin Ma - ry, The __ Queen of __ Ga - li - lee.
"Here are ap - ples, Here are cher - ries," Sweet Ma - ry __ did __ say.
"Jo - seph gath - er me some cher - ries For __ I am with __ Child."

4. Then Joseph flew in anger,
In anger flew he,
"Let the father of the Baby
Gather cherries for thee."

5. Jesus spoke a few words,
A few words spoke He,
"Give my mother some cherries,
Bow down cherry tree!

6. Bow down, cherry tree,
Low down to the ground."
Then Mary gathered cherries,
And Joseph stood around.

7. Then Joseph took Mary
All on his right knee,
"What have I done, Lord?
Have mercy on me."

8. Then Joseph took Mary
All on his left knee,
"Oh, tell me, little Baby,
When Thy birthday will be."

9. "The sixth of January
My birthday will be,
When the stars in the elements
Will tremble with glee."

'Twas in the Moon of Wintertime

ESTENNIALON DE TSONUE

Attributed to Father Jean De Brebeuf
English words by J. E. Middleton

Tune of the Wyandotte Nation
Arranged by William Llewellyn

1. 'Twas in the moon of win-ter-time, when all the birds had fled,
2. With-in a lodge of bro-ken bark, the ten-der babe was found,
2. *Es-ten-nia-lon de tson-ue Ie-sus A-ha-ton-nia,*

That might-y Git-chi Ma-ni-tou sent an-gel choirs in-stead.
A rag-ged robe of rab-bit skin en-wrapped His beau-ty round,
On-nau-a-te-ua 'd'o-ki n'on-an-dask ua-en-tak;

Be-fore their lights the stars grew dim, And wand'-ring hun-ters heard the hymn.
And, as the hun-ter braves drew nigh, The an-gel song rang loud and high.
E-non-chien sku-at-ri-ho-tat n'on-uan-dil-on-rac-hat-ha.

The Carol of the Bells

Peter J. Wilhousky

M. Leontovich

Brightly

Hark! how the bells; Sweet sil - ver bells, All seem to say, "Throw cares a - way"

Christ - mas is here Bring - ing good cheer To young and old, Meek and the bold

Ding, dong, ding, dong,

Ding, dong, ding, dong, That is their song, With joy - ful ring, All car - ol - ing.

Ding, dong, ding, dong,

One seems to hear, Words of good cheer, From ev'-ry-where Fill-ing the air

O, how they pound, Rais-ing the sound, O'er hill and dale, Tell-ing their tale,

Gay-ly they ring,— While peo-ple sing— song of good cheer,—

Continued

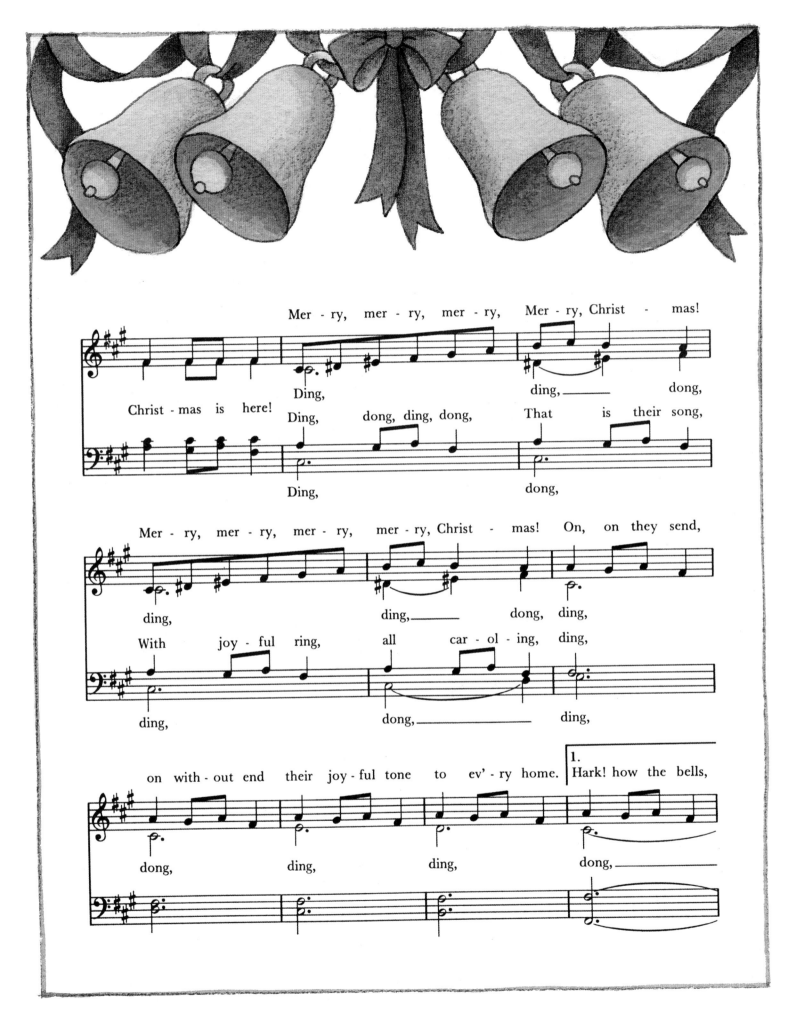

Wassail Song

Traditional

English Wassail Song

1. __ Here we come a-was-sail-ing A-mong the leaves so green; __
2. We are not dai-ly beg-gars That beg from door to door; __

__ Here we come a-wan-d'ring, So fair __ to be seen.
But we are neigh-bors' chil-dren, Whom you have seen be-fore.

Go Tell It on the Mountain

Black Spiritual

Lively

1. When I was a seek-er, I sought both night and day,
2. He made me a watch-man up-on the cit-y wall,

I sought the Lord to help me, and He showed me the way, Oh!
And if I am a Chris-tian, I am the least of all. Oh!

Refrain

Go tell it on the moun-tain, o-ver the hills and ev'-ry-where,

Go tell it on the moun-tain that Je-sus Christ_ is born!

We Wish You a Merry Christmas

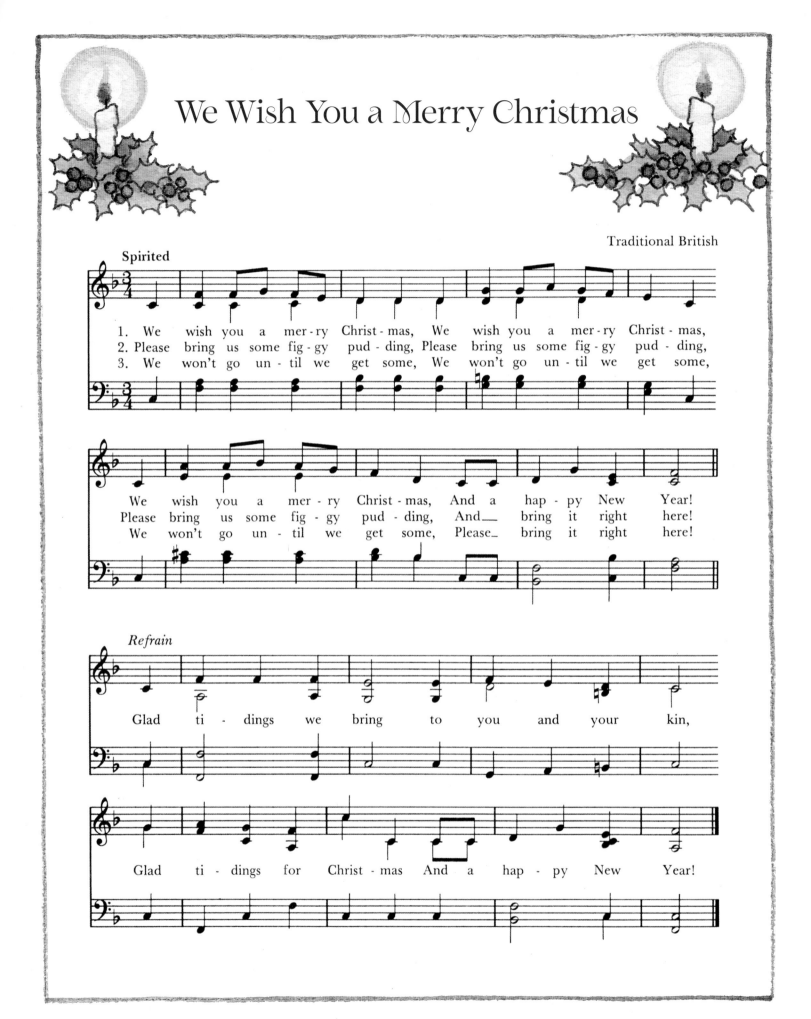

Traditional British

Spirited

1. We wish you a mer-ry Christ-mas, We wish you a mer-ry Christ-mas,
2. Please bring us some fig-gy pud-ding, Please bring us some fig-gy pud-ding,
3. We won't go un-til we get some, We won't go un-til we get some,

We wish you a mer-ry Christ-mas, And a hap-py New Year!
Please bring us some fig-gy pud-ding, And bring it right here!
We won't go un-til we get some, Please bring it right here!

Refrain

Glad ti-dings we bring to you and your kin,

Glad ti-dings for Christ-mas And a hap-py New Year!